# THE LAW OF ATTRACTION

*Your Guide to Satisfaction and Success*

Anthony Glenn

**THE LAW OF ATTRACTION:** Your Guide to Satisfaction and Success

ISBN-13: 9781723897283

Imprint: Independently published

Print & eBook Design: Glory ePublishing Services

# THE LAW OF ATTRACTION
## TABLE OF CONTENTS

# INTRODUCTION

## What if you could have or be anything you wanted?

Ask yourself what is it that what you want deep in your heart. What would your perfect life look like? Who would you want to be? How would you live? Where? With whom? How would you like your ideal partner to behave? What have you always wanted, but somehow believed was not possible? Why have you accepted the belief that you cannot achieve that, that you are not good enough, that it is not realistic? Why have you let those limiting beliefs shrink your dreams? Why do you believe that your wishes must remain wishes while you are satisfied by more reasonable substitutions?

What if all of that is not true? What if you can be or have anything, but those beliefs are what are in your way? They are only what they are: thoughts you believed in. But, you gave them power. If you choose to accept them, they become your reality. But, in the same way, you can choose something different to believe in. Anything you believe can become your reality. What is a belief? It is only a thought we have repeated enough times. What you think on repeat suddenly seems important, doesn't it?

The Law of Attraction is not here to make your wishes come true. But it is undoubtedly here, like the sun and the moon. Like gravity, it works, all the time. Be smart. Be aware of how it works, and let it help you live the life of your dreams.

## We have more power within us than we think. You are the creator.

People do not use their full brain resources and capacity. Neuroscience has not yet discovered all of the parts and functions of the brain. Through experience and intuition, we know that we have some powers that we cannot explain. So, it is not so hard to believe there are some functions we did not discover until recently.

Besides that, we sometimes feel as if we have some divine power within us. There is a power which makes your heart beat, allows you to digest your food, and causes you to breathe without even thinking about it. So, there is certainly more inside you than just your body, your thoughts, and your emotions. There is a power which can even allow you to pick up a car if a loved one is trapped under it or which allows you to do some other unbelievable thing.

We apparently have more power within us than we know. Somehow, while growing up and during schooling, we forgot about it. We were instead taught what is realistic, what is not realistic, what to believe, and what dreams to give up on. So, we forgot our true nature - who we really are. We became viewers of our reality instead of becoming the creators. Too often, we only watch things happen and then think and talk about what happened, recreating it that way.

Too often, we use our old, worn-out beliefs, which were useful when we were three years old, but which lost their function many years ago. It is time to let them go. It is time to accept the new beliefs and remind ourselves who we really are. It is time to take our creativity back, to become aware of the power within ourselves, to create an awesome reality, and to build a life worth living. The Law of Attraction will help you do just that.

# What Is the Law of Attraction?

Are you already familiar with the idea of yourself as the creator of everything in your life? Or do you still think that things just randomly happen for no specific reason? Have you heard of the universal laws and the most mighty of them all, the Law of Attraction? Here, we will simplify it to make it easier to understand.

The basic idea is that like energy attracts like energy. Everything is energy. Our bodies, our thoughts, our feelings, our experiences, the material world, the universe: it is all pure energy. Everything resonates at some vibration and attracts those things which resonate in the same way. People create their reality. We continuously attract experience through our thoughts and feelings. Negative thoughts will make you feel bad and set your vibration low so that you will attract bad experiences. On the other hand, if you think positive, supportive thoughts, you will feel good and attract those kinds of things.

The Law of Attraction is universal and works all the time. You can imagine it like gravity. It cannot be turned it off or paused. It works, believes it or not, while you are sleeping or awake, whether you are aware of it or not. Anyway, isn't it better to be aware of something like this? Think again. You are the one who creates your experiences. That means that you choose what will happen. Isn't that the best thing you have ever heard? There is an almost limitless power within you and you are the one who decides what it will do. Wow! You can use it as you like. You should use it. It has given to you for a purpose, to create your time on this planet.

## How Does It Work?

We think all the time, no matter if we are aware of it or not. Numerous thoughts pop into our minds during the day and if we have not learned how to control and choose our thoughts, our brain behaves like a dog, chasing every random thought. Many people are not even aware of having thoughts, not to mention controlling them. We will discuss choosing what you think later on. For now, it is important to understand how this all works.

Our thoughts of every kind cause feelings. There is no feeling which arises out of nowhere for no reason. Every feeling, even the tiniest, has its origin in some thought. Maybe you did not notice the thought, but it caused some feeling, and now you do not know where it came from.

Our thoughts and feelings go together like nails on fingers. They are what make us resonate at some vibration. Being there, we attract everything which resonates the same. So, if you do not like what you see in your reality, you should change what is inside of you.

It would be quite easy to change our thoughts in order to change our feelings and *voila!* experience another reality.

But in practice, it is not so simple. Why not?

Because we are not simple creatures and it is not enough to simply turn a switch as if you were changing the station on the radio.

Besides our conscious minds, we have our subconscious minds, too. We also have limiting beliefs and patterns which are more profound and stronger than any thought.

So, if we want to change the circumstances around us, we need to make a change inside of ourselves first. But, it is also important not to stay at the surface. You need to dive deep into yourself to dig up your limiting beliefs and everything which is laying in the way of the magnificent life you deserve.

There are many self-development and psychological techniques which you can use along with the Law of Attraction to achieve your highest good. Some of them come from cognitive or behavioral psychology, creative visualization, affirmations, meditation, and more. Later, we will talk more about each of them and see how you can apply them to create the life you want.

# The Five Steps in the Law of Attraction

Teachers of the Law of Attraction, as well as authors who write about it, say that there are five phases or steps one needs to take to attract the desired manifestation.

## 1. The first step is asking.

"Ask and you shall receive," says the Bible. Even though the universe is constantly responding to your vibrations, you need to request help if you want a specific manifestation. You should imagine the universe to be like a genie from the bottle, which says, "Your wish is my command." So, whatever you think or say, the genie answers, "Let it be so." If you think that to achieve anything, you have to do it all by yourself, that is how it will be. If you ask the universe for help, you will receive it. So, be wise and ask for help. Everything is much easier and more pleasant when someone has your back, especially if that is someone as powerful as the universe.

But, before you ask for support, take enough time to decide what you want. Do not waste time and energy attracting something which will not give you fulfillment. Be honest with yourself and do not try to convince yourself that you want something which others expect from you. Also, try not to fall into the trap of choosing your wishes by how likely they are to come true. It is not your job to worry about how something will happen. Your job is to find out what you truly want. What will make you happy and bring you joy? Ask your soul what it wants. Yes, that impossible dream, that is the right one. Do not limit yourself. You can choose anything, remember?

So, how it would look to live your dream life? What is the job you would like to do? When you are doing something you love, time stands still. You will never have that feeling that you have to go to work. Find your passion. Think about your perfect job: an exciting, high salary job with kind and supportive co-workers and clients surrounding you. Wouldn't that be a magical thing to look forward to on Mondays?

How would it be to meet your soulmate? That someone who is the perfect match for you, who understands you, accepts you, and loves you just the way you are? Think about the relationship you want. Imagine that person; how they look, their characteristics, the way they smile. Imagine waking up with your soul's partner, feeling loved and happy that you have found each other. Imagine your life together. You can be sure that there is indeed someone like that out there. You only need to attract them into your reality.

If you have some health issue, imagine how it would be to be perfectly healthy again. Wouldn't it be magnificent to have a healthy body which could serve you for many more years? If you have a diagnosis, wouldn't it be the best to hear from your doctor, "Your problem is gone. You are perfectly healthy"? You can beat that illness. You can run. You can enjoy food and drinks. You can smile with your friends, play with your children or grandchildren, and you can still enjoy life.

Maybe you want to become a parent, but some obstacles lay in your way. Or your priority is to win some contest, to become an actor, to buy a house, to move to another place... anything. Think about your dreams, your desires, and your priorities. Maybe you have many wishes. Start with the most important. Or, maybe you would prefer to begin with small wishes and then build up to bigger ones. That is okay, too.

Just define what you want. Be honest, precise, and specific. For example, if you wish to have money, it is better to specify the amount than to try and attract money in general. If you are not specific, do not blame the Law of Attraction if the universe sends you the totally wrong guy with a great sense of humor, for example. You will get what you order, so do not leave it to chance.

## 2. It is already given in your vortex or parallel reality.

This may be difficult to understand at first. Imagine a virtual space, another reality, in which everything is perfect for you, just as you wish. Everything you desire is there. That is your vortex. When you want something and ask the universe, it gives you what you want immediately. Everything you want is already provided. "But wait," you say, "why can't I see it?" That is because you are the one who is not at the same vibration as your desired manifestation. You need to believe before you can see. You need to raise your vibration to get to experience what you asked for. Raising your vibration is crucial when trying to attract something.

If you believe that what you want is somewhere nearby and you need just a little to see it at your fingertips, it is easier to feel it, to be happy, excited, and thankful for it. Being grateful for something which is yet to come is the best way to tell the universe that you believe in it. You know for sure that what you want is on its way as if you had ordered it from an online shop. You do not have to worry about if they will send you what you have requested or not. You can relax and have fun, knowing that everything is going to be just fine.

### 3. *Allowing: Get out of the way to your manifestations. Set your thoughts and emotions to make your vibrations match your desires.*

What does this mean? It means you need to move out of the way of your manifestations. Let them happen. If you think that you do not sabotage them, think again. That is impossible. How on Earth will that happen? When? How long do I have to wait? Can it happen now? What about now? Well, I knew it. It's impossible. Does that sound familiar? And what about your emotions? If you feel as if you are going to fly from excitement in one moment and then find yourself depressed in the next, what happens to your vibration? It goes up and down, too high then too low, constantly missing the vibration for everything you want. You need to set your vibration to match your desires. How can you do that? By choosing your emotions and feeling good. How can you choose what to feel? By selecting your thoughts. To feel awesome, you need to think positive, lovely thoughts. Think about your desired outcomes. Send them love. Be happy about the future that is about to come. Be excited about all the gifts, but also think about the present with love and gratitude. It is not so much about what you think, it is more important how you feel because that will determine what you attract. So, it will have the same, good effect if you focus on some other thing which makes you happy: a hobby, recreation, hanging out with friends, playing with children, or spending time with a pet. The point is to feel splendid. That is how you get to a higher vibration and maintain it.

And the other, equally important thing is to get out of the way. Your manifestation wants to reach you, but it cannot because of your negative thoughts and attitude, because you are not available, because you are on some other vibration, or because you will not let it come close. Move out of the way.

Leave yourself open for good things to happen. Accept new, positive thoughts and views. Make an effort to replace your old beliefs with new ones. Set your attitude to positive and expect miracles. If your desire is too strong and it makes you feel anxious or anything other than happy, change your focus. Do something else. Do some gardening or make a pie. Focus your attention on small things. The big ones will take care of themselves anyway.

## 4. Unconditional: Realize that you do not need manifestations to be happy.

In Step 3: Allowing, you learned how to get to a high vibration. You know how great you feel there. Also, you notice when you fall off of it. You know what actions to take to get back. Now, when you have learned how to feel good, you can see how the conditions impact you. When something is not as you would like, you do not think it is a catastrophe but know it is a contrast. This is a natural part of the process. It is here to teach you more about what you want and what you do not want. You can feel good no matter what. Conditions can change, but they do not have to. Now you are choosing how to feel unconditionally. What a freedom it is not to depend on circumstances! Your manifestation could happen or not happen, and you will be happy either way. This is the point at which you realize that you do not need it. You want it, but you do not need it to be happy.

## 5. Welcome contrast.

In the Law of Attraction, contrast is anything you do not want. Life is full of contrasts and you have already experienced them for sure. They are also a natural part of life and the world. That is how all desires are born. There is nothing wrong with contrast. But, people are often afraid of it and want to avoid it.

Why? Contrast is unpleasant. But that is its purpose: bringing clarity. That is how you find out what you want and what you do not want. It brings space for growth and expansion. Without contrast, all beautiful things would not exist. Neither would wishes be born. There would not be expansion, clarity, or self-growth. There would not be the conditions needed for conscious waking.

Now, after you have mastered the first four steps, you will realize this. And you will be ready to welcome contrast. You can bless it and be thankful for the opportunities it brings. You will not be afraid of anything anymore, because you know that they are lessons. And when you live on a high vibration, you know how to prevent any unwanted thing from happening.

# How to Attract Anything You Want

That is all good and nice, but how do you apply that to real life? Let's see how you can use the five steps we have discussed to manifest what you want.

### Wishes: *Be sure of what you want.*

As we have already mentioned, the first step is to be clear about what you want. Although you may think this is something that everybody knows for themselves, do not skip this step. Too often, we just think we want something. But, what you genuinely desire may be significantly different from what you think you want. How so? We are taught what we should wish for, what we should become, and what we should do with our lives. But many times, even if we achieve those things, it turns out that they were not what our soul was calling for. So, take some time to reflect on what you want. Is it really your original wish or did someone tell you that you should do that? Would it make you happy? Deep inside, you already know the answer. Be honest with yourself and let the real answers be heard.

For example, you may think that you wish to finally finish your law studies. But that is actually something that your parents want, while you would rather become a writer. Or your priority is to get married and start a family, while your true desire would be to get on a bike and cycle around the world instead. That is what we mean when we say to be honest with yourself.

## Ask the universe for help.

We have mentioned this one, too. It is a huge benefit to have the mighty universe at your back. If you believe you are divinely protected and being guided towards your highest good, nothing can stop you. Simply ask the universe to give you what you want. You can say it out loud if you would like or mentally if that is more pleasant for you. You can conceptualize your request as a prayer. That is okay, too. If you are most comfortable with a pen and paper, write a letter. That works as well. The point is to ask the universe, for real, in any way you would like. If the universe had a phone or an email address, that would be okay, too. Leave the jokes aside and ask, no matter how silly it may seem. And afterward, behave as if you have ordered something from a real shop and wait for your manifestation to arrive. Be excited. Be happy. Be patient. Be full of faith.

## Write down your dreams.

Do you know what abracadabra means? It is believed to come from a phrase in Hebrew that means, "I will create as I speak," or from the Aramaic, "I create like the word." So, some kind of magic happens when we write. Seriously, it has been scientifically proven that written goals have more of a chance of becoming reality. The same thing applies to wishes we want to manifest. When writing, our conscious and subconscious minds focus on our thoughts and our energy flows where our attention goes. All of these are tools for attraction. Besides, written words on paper are a kind of first material manifestation of an idea. So, if you have written something down, you have already manifested it in one way, no matter how small. This begins the transition from the immaterial to the material world.

So, get a pen and paper and have fun with writing out your

new life scenario. Set your imagination free and do not limit yourself. The only criteria should be your own good feelings.

## *Feel it.*

It is not enough to keep an eye on your thoughts and select them carefully. Even creatively writing your new story is not enough. The crucial thing is to feel it. You will attract those things that are on the same vibration as your feelings. When you feel great, you are flying high and are attracting awesome manifestations like a magnet. In short, you are creating with your feelings. Imagination and thoughts are given to you to cause emotions which in turn determine your vibration. So, imagine how you would feel if your wish were to come true. Try to feel as if it has already happened. These are the emotions which will help you attract more of the same feelings by bringing wanted manifestations into your reality. Remember, it is not important what you do, but how you feel. Do whatever makes you feel wonderful. And choose your thoughts wisely, selecting only those which make you feel good.

## *What should you do with your beliefs?*

We all believe many things about life and the world. Many of them are correct and useful. For example, it is dangerous to play with fire. This kind of thought is rational. Our beliefs can be supportive, like if you think you are gorgeous and talented. In proper doses, this can be good for your self-esteem. But, not all of our beliefs are lovely, supportive, or rational. While most adults do not believe that Santa Claus exists, for some reason we often believe equally silly things that we were taught when we were three. You can try to use positive thinking and mindfulness, but if you have limiting beliefs working against you, you will have no chance. So, is there any hope? Of course, there is. We all have some limiting beliefs and if we do not do anything about them our autopilot will be a three-year-old. Your beliefs just need some special attention and decluttering. First, you need to be clear about what you believe. What do you think is undoubtedly true about life, about yourself, about other people, and about the world? What do you think about love, friendship, and family? What do you think about money and work? How do you feel about all of these topics? Take as much time as you need for deep introspection and reflection on each of those themes. Dig deep into your beliefs and see if they serve you. If a belief is true, rational, supportive, or makes you feel good, it is helpful. If it limits, sabotages, or discourages you, it is not useful. It is time to get rid of toxic beliefs and to accept new ones instead.

## Affirmations can help.

When you have realized that you need to change some of your beliefs, affirmations are your secret weapon. These are positive, declarative sentences. For this purpose, there is no more powerful way. It is important for a good affirmation to be formulated in the present tense and, most often, in the first person. For example, "I am loved. I am peaceful. I am a money magnet." You can find numerous affirmations out there, but you could and should create your own. For every belief that you want to change, create a new one that is positive and supportive, and formulate it as an affirmation. Then you simply need to repeat it until you accept it as your new belief. The first hour in the morning and the last one before you fall asleep are perfect for affirmations.

How does this work? Our subconscious does not judge and cannot differentiate true from false. It does not know the difference between what is real and what is imagined. Our beliefs are only the thoughts we chose to believe once. They were just repeated enough times. Everything that you continuously repeat becomes your belief and tends to prove itself. This is not magic, it is psychology. This is how our minds work and why affirmations will change your life. Just formulate what you want, repeat it again and again, and let the universe make it your new reality.

### *Vibrations: Reach the right one.*

You already know that to attract what you want, you need to raise your vibration. All of the methods and techniques for self-improvement and attraction have this in common: their primary purpose is to increase one's vibration. The only way to have a high vibration and to keep it there is to feel good - or even better - to feel great. Everything you love to do or like to think about, everything which makes you happy raises your vibration. You can achieve this by choosing only positive thoughts. For example, if you only think of things you adore, you will emit so many positive waves that all you want will hurry to reach you. The basic techniques to raise your vibration are thought control (thinking in the best possible way by choosing only those thoughts which are good for you), focusing with purpose, and gratefulness. So, if you want to feel better now, think about the things which make your life special and worthwhile. Think about your loved ones, the wonderfulness of the world, or watch funny animal videos. What is important is not what you do, but how you feel. Choose to do more of what makes you happy and adapt your schedule to those priorities, not the other way around. Focus intentionally on the bright side of everything. There is always a sunny side. Find it and keep it in the spotlight. And, finally, count your blessings. Look at how lucky you are and say thank you.

## Use the power of focus.

Energy flows where attention goes. What you focus your attention on, that you grow. So, what things in your life do you want to grow and cultivate, and which of them are better to be left out of your garden? Your focus is similar to a camera lens. Be careful what you choose to include in your life movie. Focusing on what you like and what you would be glad to have more of in your reality makes you feel good. Everything will look better and, by the Law of Attraction, you will bring more similar experiences, things, and people to your life. We are not saying that you should ignore problems which demand action. But, there are many things which only deplete your energy. Focusing on them leaves you drained and in a bad mood. These are the things which should not be given a place in your movie. The healthiest thing for your vibration is not to bring them with you. Put a mental "ignore" sign on them and change your focus. After some practice, you will be pleasantly surprised by how easy it is to shift your focus and to be intentional in choosing your thoughts and feelings.

## Gratefulness.

Being grateful is the most powerful and quickest way to jump up to high vibration. It is an instant way to feel good. It is easy, quick, totally free, and entirely under your control. The technique is incredible and your job is to apply it. Think about all the things in your life you could be thankful for. What would you miss if you lost it? Be grateful for life, for your body, its parts, and its function. You can be thankful for your mind, for your imagination, for your intelligence, for your brain, for beautiful days, for sunlight, for all of the precious people in your life, for your bed, for a cup of coffee, for whatever makes your life easier or more beautiful. Everybody who is alive has a lot to be grateful for. Everything above and beyond that is an additional bonus. We are fortunate to be here. It is like we have won the lottery. But unfortunately, many of us are not aware of this. Count your blessings whenever you can. Do it in the morning to raise your vibration for a new day, before bedtime to program your subconscious, or during the day just to feel good. When you are thankful for whatever you already have, you are attracting more of the same vibration. If you like to write thankful notes, even better. You can start a gratefulness diary or a happiness jar. These are interesting projects which will remind you every day to say thanks for what you have. In the end, when the project is finished, it will also tell you how lucky you are every time you look at. For the happiness jar, you will need a big, empty jar and a lot of little pieces of paper. Every day, write down one thing you are thankful for and put it in the jar. This is so simple, but effective. Your jar will be a reminder for you and a magnet to attract more pieces of paper with wonderful things written on them.

### *Practice creative visualization.*

We have already said that our mind is ruled by two masters: our conscious mind and our subconscious mind. We can be aware of that fact or not, but when our mind receives an order, it does not know or care which one it comes from. That is why it can be tricky to understand all of our emotions and actions. But, you can make use of this. You will attract what you want most easily if you feel like it has already happened. Because our minds do not care if something is real or imagined, you can easily trick them. By imagining your wanted scenario, you will feel as if it has already occurred. In this way, you will realize that you do not need the manifestation to achieve those emotions and, more importantly, the universe will send you more reasons to stay on your current vibration. This is the point of creative visualization. What you need to do is to imagine the scenario you have wished for. Be creative and pay attention to details. You need to create a picture you would believe. Your mind is clever, do not forget that. If you want to provoke feelings, you need to put in some effort and be imaginative. Imagine situations, things, people, their reactions, smell, taste, touch, your actions, and your feelings. Imagine everything you can. All of this is needed to feel the emotion. Emotions are what vibrate and attract, so that is our goal. The point of creative visualization is to provoke the adequate emotion which will attract more.

## Create your new story.

People often talk about their experiences, especially those that they do not like. In that way, by talking about yesterday, they will create their today and tomorrow. This creates a never-ending circle: the same story creates the same experiences that they will talk about to create the same thing yet again. If you want to change something and attract something new, you need to change the story you tell. It is time to make up a new story. This is similar to creative visualization. You need to imagine the whole story you would like to live. Pay attention to what you are constantly talking about. Are you complaining a lot? Are there things you do not like or do not want? You can write them down, too, if that is easier for you. Then replace every single sentence with a new one. Write out your new reality. Imagine that you will live everything that you write down. And then let yourself be limitlessly imaginative. Do not limit your ideas to how possible they are. The crazier, the better. Again, the feeling is what we are looking for. Once you accept your new story and start talking about it instead of the old one, your reality will change accordingly.

### *Meditation.*

Meditation is an excellent method for curing almost everything. It is a real miracle how much you can get by doing nothing in that way. Meditation has numerous benefits for our health, our bodies, our minds, and our souls. And it is incredibly easy to practice. You need almost nothing to begin. A place to sit will be enough. And breathing, but you already do that. Start small and simple. The results will amaze you.

When you relax your whole body in meditation and calm your mind, all resistance will disappear. You will be ready to accept everything you want. Here is the thing: there are too many thoughts that pop up into our minds all the time. If you let them grab your attention, they will run around like a dog and will make you have different feelings at almost every moment. So, your vibration will be chaotic and inconsistent.

In meditation, we obtain clearness about what we want and are able to keep our focus on that. We also learn how to easily get rid of what we do not want and how to ignore distractions. When we are calm, clear-minded, and relaxed, we will be ready to attract and accept what is for our highest good.

Meditating will help you with the other techniques as well. You will become more in control of your mind and more intentional in choosing your thoughts and what you focus on. You will be aware of every thought that arises and the feelings it provokes. You will immediately know if it is something you want to attract or not.

So, start with meditation as soon as you can. In the beginning, start with short sessions of five minutes. Find some quiet place, sit still, and concentrate on your breath. That is enough to start with.

### Be present in the moment.

Yes, the Law of Attraction is all about creating the future, but do not forget one more important fact: it is happening now. Your creation of some future experiences is happening right now. So, if you imagine some better version of yourself in the future who is attracting better things, stop. You, you in the present, are the only one who thinks, feels, and creates. Do not just wait for tomorrow to bring you manifestations while you try to skip the present. Manifestations may come or may not come, but you will undoubtedly miss out on some days of your life. That is a shame because the creation should be fun. And, one more thing you might have forgotten: you will not attract what you want if you feel bad now. The crucial thing is how you feel at this very moment. That is how you vibrate. That is how you attract. Do everything you can to feel good now.

Be completely present in every moment and you will feel the fullness of life. That is how the magic starts to happen. Everything you want will be on the way to you because the universe will give you more moments to enjoy.

If you do not know how to be happy now or how to enjoy this and every moment, you will not know if all your wishes come true, because then it will be "now," too.

### Be what you want to attract.

We have already said that the main principle of the Law of Attraction is that similarities attract. How do you think you would you attract love if you did not feel it? How can you create abundance when you are thinking about poverty? Try to grow within yourself what you want to see around you. Be the source of what you want to accept. Give others what you want to have more of. If you want to be loved, love first. If you wish for riches, be generous. Everybody has something to give, it does not have to be money or even material goods. Give what you have: your time, your attention, your smiles, and your kindness. That is how you tell the universe, "I have a lot of this. I don't need it, but I am happy that I have it. Thank you." Then you will get more of it because you are sharing with the world. The good from helping multiplies. If you want to heal, be the cure for someone else's illness or pain.

## *Trust the process and be patient.*

Believing means that you trust even without seeing. Attraction is one of those things. Being suspicious and impatient will make you vibrate on an entirely different frequency than you should if you want to attract good. Being calm and knowing everything you want is on the way makes you feel excited and expect beautiful things to happen. If you believe that you are divinely protected and guided, you feel safe and know that you can have everything which is right for you. If something is not happening, you know the obstacles are blessings that are for a higher good, too. Remember, the universe answers your thoughts like a genie from a bottle. Whatever you choose to believe, it responds, "Let it be so." So, choose to have help and everything will be much easier. Impatience is a sign that you do not believe. Be peaceful and wait patiently for your manifestation to become visible. Believing also means that you are sure that things will happen at the perfect time for you. There is no need to rush, the universe knows best when the time is right. Silence your ego a bit. You are not the one who knows what is the best for you. You do not know what should happen nor how nor when. Let the universe make those decisions. You must enjoy life in perfect harmony.

# MANIFESTATION WITHOUT ACTION: IS IT POSSIBLE?

We will answer this immediately: yes and no. Need more of an explanation? Okay, then just keep on reading.

Are you one of those people who think that the Law of Attraction is here to make your wishes come true? That it should be something like a reward you earned for knowing the big secret? You have found out about the law, read a few books about it, and now you deserve a prize for being an expert. So, now you can relax at home and do nothing because you have your genie in the bottle. It is enough to simply make up what you want, demand it, and *voila!* everything is in front of you on a silver platter. Well, we agree it should be simple. And it is okay to take a break sometimes. But, do not be disappointed if you realize that you are attracting more reasons for doing nothing, more time at home, more wishes, and more people who got it all wrong.

That is because the Law of Attraction is not here for you and your wishes. You have not found a magic lamp. It is a universal law, like gravity. It works as it works, all of the time, and is not dependent on you or on anyone else. We are talking about being aware of it and being wise enough to use it. You need to learn smart ways to make it work for you.

Let's start at the beginning. What does the phrase "without action" mean to you? Does it mean "without any action" or "without too much effort"? Or does it mean something else entirely?

If what you would like the most is to get what you want without even trying, why is that? Why do you want to avoid action? Are actions unpleasant for you? Would you like to do something else instead? What else would you do? Think about it for a moment. Maybe your activity or goal is not suitable for you. Do you want what you say you want? Go back to the step where you defined your wishes. Be honest. Maybe what you wished for is not your real passion. When you do what you love, it feels like butterflies in your stomach and it makes you excited to wake up. If you think you are just too lazy to work on your dreams, maybe they are not your dreams. People are rarely lazy. Too often, they are unmotivated. When you find what drives you and motivates you from the depths of your soul, you will not avoid action anymore. Every step, even an unpleasant one, becomes a part of a more significant, meaningful picture.

The other thing to do if you would like to achieve your goals without struggling and trying too hard is to do so under constant pressure. Here the Law of Attraction can help you. If you use it along with your focused efforts, it will accelerate your success. There is a huge difference between taking action from a low vibration and taking it from a high vibration. If you are on a high vibration, everything you do has more of a chance to succeed. So, it is crucial to raise your vibration first and then take action.

When you are resonating positively, you will meet different people, be given different chances, see or hear different things, and take different actions than if you were trying to do something from a low vibration.

Now comes the crucial part of this question: what is an action to you? That is what the final answer depends on. Do you think that taking action means that you have to go somewhere, find someone or something, communicate with certain people, make some phone calls, or take significant steps on the outside? Then the answer for you is yes. Yes, it is possible to attract manifestations without taking those kinds of actions. The right people will find you and the right things will happen in the perfect moment if you are on the right vibration. That is where you should be to attract what you want.

And here we are. To be on the right vibration, you will need action. That demands work and effort. If you think you can achieve this without any effort, either physical or mental, the answer for you is no. Attracting manifestation without that kind of action is impossible. Maybe you do not have to cross the world to find the right person and the right answer, but you do have to get your butt off the sofa, turn off the TV, and go meditate. You have to change your mental switch and choose your thoughts. You need to learn how to be in control of your focus. You are the one who needs to put a lot of effort into self-development and learning how to use the Law of Attraction. No one can do it for you. Why did you assume that practicing all of these methods and techniques is not an action? Maybe you have not tried them yet. Now is the perfect time to begin.

# How to Attract Money

Now, we will apply everything we talked about using a real, particular example.

Wealth, love, health, and joy: these are the things people often search for. That is why we will start here and talk about attracting those things. But you can apply all of this to anything you want, any situation or relationship.

After reading this, you will have a more precise guideline of what exactly to do with your new knowledge.

Let's begin first of all with wealth.

- *Define what you want and be precise.* How much money do you want? How much would be enough for the lifestyle you are dreaming of? Do not be lazy, calculate it. What is the amount you wish to have on a regular basis? Monthly, for example. Make it clear. I want *this precise amount* of money in my account, this much in my wallet, that much in my possession, and this quantity in my piggy bank. If you wish to get some unexpected money from any source, be precise. If you do not make things clear, a single penny could also be the answer to your wish.

- *Ask the universe.* Money is energy, like everything else. There is a limitless amount of it in the universe. Feel free to ask for it. Do not be shy about wanting it. Many of us have biases related to money. We are taught that it is not right to want it. That is why we hesitate to attract money. You have been sent to this world to enjoy its fullness and abundance, not to struggle and look at it from a distance. The universe gives you what you want, depending on how you vibrate.

- *Write down your wishes.* Write it down as if it has already come true. So, do not write a general, "I wish for this much money," but rather something like, "I have this much money" or "I have received this much money." Write it in the present tense as an affirmative sentence and be precise. You can also write a check to yourself from the universe. Be creative and make it fun. Try out different things. The goal is to feel like the money is on its way to you and that you are rich.

-*Feel it.* Yes, it can be hard to feel differently from how you currently feel, but it is crucial because this dictates how you are attracting. If you think about poverty and worry about money, that is what you will create. You need to feel abundance and the fullness of this life as if you were already rich. Practicing all of these techniques will help you to do that. The point is to make yourself feel as you need to feel to create what you want.

- *Change your beliefs.* If you do not live in affluence then you surely have some limiting beliefs about it. That is not surprising because almost all people have them. Civilization has taught us that money is bad. Many religions propagate the same. We will not go into more depth to explain this, but you need to know that you are not alone and that it is perfectly normal to have biases about money. What you need to do is to think more about what your biases are. Dig deep into your beliefs about money. Be honest and merciless. *Money is the root of all evil. Money makes people bad. Money spoils people. Money often costs too much. Money and love do not go together.* The list goes on and on to eternity. What are your biases? When you have detected them, you should be aware that those are what stops you and keeps money away from you. You need to change them. But, how?

- *Use affirmations.* For every negative belief, there is a cure, an affirmation. This is the same as when writing your wishes, you need first person affirmative sentences in the present tense which make you feel good. Repeat them enough times and they will become your new beliefs which will create a new reality. You can make up your own affirmations or borrow them from a book or the internet. The options are limitless. You just need to discover what works for you and best eliminates your harmful programming. Some of the most well-known affirmations about money include:

*Money comes to me easily and frequently.*

*I'm a money magnet.*

*Money comes to me in both expected and unexpected ways.*

- *Reach the right vibration.* Everything which makes you feel rich and glamorous is welcome. Also, everything which helps you to spot the abundance around you and to be aware of how colorful, full, and rich life is. When you do something you enjoy, even if it has nothing to do with wealth, you raise your vibration and attract all good, abundance included.

- *Use the power of focus to attract money.* Focus on what you already have. Make a habit of counting your blessings. Be grateful for every coin which comes to you. Always focus on what you have instead of what you lack.

-*Nothing is as powerful as being grateful.* If abundance is what you are seeking, that becomes even more obvious. Start right now. Remind yourself of at least five things you are thankful for. There will certainly be many more and you will prolong your list every time you think about it. When these thoughts include money and material goods, include them in your grateful mode. Do not forget to give thanks for all of your possessions, for all of the money that comes to you, and all the money that you have. Money is energy. It does not like to stand still. It must flow. So, if you are trying to keep a hold on money, it will not be pleased. You are upsetting its flow. Relax and let the money go. It will be thankful and will most likely come back to you. Mentally say, "Thank you. I love you. I am happy to let you go. Come back to me multiplied." Feel grateful for every bit of money in every shape, even the pennies that you find on the street. Do not be surprised if you begin to notice many more of them. That is the first sign that your money channels are opening.

- *Now, close your eyes and imagine that you have a lot of money.* Imagine that you won the lottery or got the money from some other unexpected source. You have a limitless amount. How do you feel? Let yourself feel that excitement and that relief because you will not have to worry about money anymore. Imagine your new life with its new possibilities. Imagine the faces of your loved ones when you tell them what happened as you give them so much money that they are shocked. Imagine what it means to them, too. Imagine that you have absolutely everything that you have ever wanted. You can do anything and travel anywhere on the globe. Feel as if all of this is happening right now. Let yourself believe that all of that is real. Do not hold on to reality as you see it. Remember, your subconscious does not care if it is real or imagined. Neither does the universe.

*Start telling your new story.* You are the central character in your story, but with a lot of money. What would you do with that power? Let your imagination run free, be creative, and have fun. Where do you travel in this story? Who do you help? Be as imaginative as you can. The goal is to free yourself from your imagined limits and boundaries.

Also, if in your everyday conversations you are often someone who complains about not having enough, stop it. Share the other story. Talk as if you are someone who is on the way to becoming the character of your new story. If *"I am rich. I have a lot of money.*" does not sound true, you do not have to lie. Just change your point of view to something like "*Things are better for me every day. I have more and more. Every day I am a little closer to my dream.*"

- *Relax your entire body in meditation for at least fifteen minutes per day.* This will relieve all of your blockades which stand in the way of your abundance. You can also find guided meditations for attracting wealth to try out.

-*Remain calm and feel assured that you will soon experience abundance.* You just need to be patient. Soon all of your worries about money will soon be in the past.

# How to Attract Love

Everyone wants to love and be loved in return. This is a basic human need. And there are very few things which can compare to this. Why, then, do so many people have problems in this field? For some of them, it seems almost impossible to find an adequate partner. Others have difficulties maintaining a relationship. For many, it is hard to open their hearts to someone because they have been hurt in the past. Where are all of these problems coming from? Maybe you were abandoned or not loved enough during childhood. Perhaps you received negative thoughts, programming, or patterns of love from your family. Maybe they were hurt, too, and taught you that love hurts. Whatever it is, you can get rid of it. You can find love. You deserve to love and be loved.

**How?**

Be the love. Before anything else, when it comes to love, you need to be the source of what you want to receive. Be a source of pure, unconditional love for everyone and everything. Love yourself, love life, and love other people. Find some loving thought in your heart for everything. It is impossible not to be loved when you are the embodiment of love!

Define the love that you want. What do you wish for exactly? How do you want to love? How do you want to be loved? How do you want your partner to show you their love? How do you want to feel? How do you want to be treated? If you would like to improve a relationship that you already have, be precise about what you want and how it should be. If you are seeking a partner, be clear about what you are searching for.

Define how your partner should behave, how they should look, and what values and opinions you should share. How would you like your relationship to go? And how about a usual day together?

Ask the universe to send you the right person. If there is that one, they are searching for you, too. Ask the universe to act as your matchmaker. The universe likes to have fun, too. That is why the world is such a fun place.

Write your wish down. You can write it as if it is already true. Add a date to make it timelier and more precise. For example, "December/DD/YYYY: I am in a happy relationship." Let yourself be creative.

Feel how loved you are. There is probably more than one person who loves you: your parents, grandparents, children, aunts, uncles, friends, your friends' children, your dog, your cat. It does not matter who, but you are loved. You are also a beloved child of the universe. It loves you unconditionally. Feel the love that you have for others. Who do you love? Your mom, your dad, your sibling, but who else? The goal is to feel the energy of love, commitment, and connection. You can also feel the love between other people. For example, when you see a happy couple on the street, try to imagine how they feel. Or the emotion which a young mom with a stroller feels towards her baby. This will allow those to become your feelings as well so that you vibrate with love. And then - you guessed it! - you will attract love.

Take some time for reflection and introspection. Think about your beliefs about love. Dig into the deepest ones. If you do not have a wonderful relationship that you are entirely satisfied with, you undoubtedly have some limiting beliefs about love. Bring them out into the daylight. It is time to say goodbye to them.

Replace them with your soon-to-be beliefs: with affirmations. There are plenty of affirmations about love and relationships. Again, you can create your own or use some that already exist. Choose those that are most applicable to your case. Here are some of the most well-known:

*I am worthy of love. I deserve to be loved.*
*I love myself and the people around me.*
*Others show me love so that I can feel it.*
*I attract loving and caring people.*
*My partner and I are both happy together. Our relationship is joyous.*
*I happily give and receive love each day.*

By using affirmations, thinking loving thoughts, focusing on the love around and inside of you, being grateful for all of the love in the universe, and becoming a source of love, you will undoubtedly reach your love vibration. Bless everything you do and everyone you see with love, mentally. Wherever you go, send love ahead of you. Then love will be what you attract, always.

Keep your focus on love. Notice it everywhere. Do not skip over it and pay attention to hate, loneliness, or misery. In every human being, there is enough love to make the world go round. Just keep your focus on that.

Feel grateful for all the love in the world, for the love you feel for others, and for the love you get from them. Be thankful for all the support and guidance you receive from the universe. Be grateful for every hug and kiss from your child, grandparent, or anyone else, even for the cheerful barking of your dog when you return home.

Use your imagination to visualize everything. Imagine your perfect relationship, your everyday life together, how you feel, what you do together, and so on. Imagine the one and their smile as you sip coffee together on the balcony. Add as many details as you can imagine. The more, the better. Make yourself feel like as if it is happening in real time so that you vibrate with love and togetherness.

Write down the romance that you visualized so that you can reread it every time you need to raise your vibration.

If you used to talk about loneliness and complain about romantic difficulties, stop. Change this to a new, better story, or do not talk about that subject at all.

Meditation will help you here, also. When you are absolutely relaxed and focused on your breathing or other sounds, your blockades will disappear so that love can finally find you.

Be patient, again. Your ideal partner needs some time to reach to you. Be sure that it will happen when the time is right for both of you.

# How to Use the Law of Attraction to Heal Yourself

Maybe you have heard that you are the one who has the power to heal your body. Most authors, teachers, doctors, and scientists agree about one thing: the human body has the potential to heal itself. That is how placebos work, how we recover, and how many people overcome illnesses that seem to have no cure. That is how miracles happen.

What is surprising is that they also say that all of our health problems come from our minds. Some of our negative thoughts and beliefs are so toxic that they harm our bodies. The illness is not the main problem, but rather a symptom of a deeper problem.

You can even find long lists of health problems and the negative beliefs which lead to them.

How can you possibly be doing that to yourself?

No one wants to get sick. You are not self-destructive on purpose. It is your subconscious which is working against you. In one word, you do not love yourself enough. That means that you have negative thoughts and beliefs about yourself, like "I'm not good enough." "I'm too fat / skinny / tall / short / ugly / stupid," or whatever else you think about yourself. We are talking about that negative voice in your head which you hear when you look into the mirror, after having a conversation, or anytime you think about yourself. We all came to this world as babies who adored themselves and their bodies, knowing exactly how precious and divine they were. But growing up, we learned that we were not so perfect, that we could not do what we wanted, that we were not worthy, and so on. We forgot how to love ourselves unconditionally.

Now, if you have some negative diagnoses, it is your final chance to change and to fall in love with yourself. This is the only real cure and it is more powerful and durable than any medical solution.

You already know that you want to be healed, right? Just define your wish and ask the universe for help. You can also say a prayer to the universe, angels, God, or whatever else you believe in. Decide to be divinely protected and guided through the healing process and ask for it to happen. Then be carefree and full of trust. Someone more powerful than you is leading your recovery.

Meanwhile, you need to dig into your toxic beliefs and replace them with affirmations. Repeat your affirmations at least three times per day, as if you were taking a medication. Some examples affirmations include:

"*I deserve to be perfectly healthy.*"
"*Every cell in my body is healthy.*"
"*I feel energy and vitality in every part of my body.*"
"*I feel better every day.*"

If you have not tried meditation yet, make it a new habit. The more you manage to relax and meditate, the faster your healing will be. Every cell in your body will benefit from meditation. Try out some of the many guided meditations for relaxing and healing. The goal is to relax the entire body part by part, by focusing on each part one at a time. The next step is focusing on breathing while imaging white, healing light curing your body with every breath that you take.

Use the time you have to spend in bed or at home calmly visualizing your wanted results. Imagine your life after being cured. Enjoy it. Feel it. Feel health and energy in every part of your body. Visualize your doctor telling you that you are completely cured and totally healthy. Let yourself feel all the excitement and happiness as if it is happening for real.

Do not talk about your problems. Instead, choose some other subject to chat about. If someone asks you how are you, answer with how you want to be instead of how you sincerely are if how you are is not so good.

No matter what is happening, keep your focus on the bright side. Focus on your health improvement, even if it is going slowly in small steps. Do not think about any other options, but only about healing. Focus on your "why." Why do you have to be cured? Why do you want to live a long, happy, and healthy life? Why you need your body to serve you properly for much more time? Focus on the good in life, in people, in yourself, in your body, and in every possible thing.

Be grateful for every single day. In illness, people often realize how precious their health is and how magical it is to be alive. Use that experience for self-growth and take as much as you can from it. Make it your life lesson, which will make you stronger with unstoppable happiness. Be thankful for your body, every part of it and its functions. Feel grateful for the health you have, for every health part and everything that goes well in your body. And do not forget to be thankful for every person and thing which makes your life worth living. Write a gratefulness journal where you can write about happy moments and about your healing, so that you can reread it whenever you feel the need to raise your vibration.

Believe in the wisdom of nature, in the divine power which protects you and guides you, and in your body. Trust your body, and know it will heal itself. You just need to help it a bit by controlling your mind.

By using these pieces of advice, you will raise your vibration to attract health and harmony. The healing process will be faster and the results better.

Do everything you can, but do not take your illness too seriously. It is here to serve you as a challenge and an opportunity for growth. Be patient, love yourself, and have fun with the Law of Attraction. And do not forget to smile.

# If You Are a Skeptic

Now, when you have read all of these methods, you will know how to use the Law of Attraction and will be able to apply it to your particular situation. Are you going to test it? What do you feel is often more accurate than what you think about something? Listen to your inner being. Is it telling you there indeed is something about this Law Of Attraction? Or are you a skeptic? If so, let's first look at what that means. In the dictionary, a skeptic is defined as "a person inclined to question or doubt accepted opinions." Well, that is not bad at all. Of course, you should have an inquisitive mind. It is good to use your mind creatively: to doubt, to test, to ask questions. That is how we grow as people. This is what a skeptic does. They do not believe everything they hear or read but like to examine and test things.

If you do not just want to try to use the Law of Attraction, that is okay, too. But that is not about the Law, it is about you. Do not call yourself a skeptic or blame the Law for not working. You just do not want to try. Perhaps you have your own ways and beliefs that serve you. If you are happy with your life, that is wonderful. That is the primary goal we are all trying to reach and everybody does it in their own way.

All of you are more than welcome to try out and test all of the advice in this book. The only thing which could happen to you is that you accidentally grow as a person and become happier during the test period. But that is quite the acceptable risk, right?

# OTHER BOOKS BY
# ANTHONY GLENN

**Mental Hygiene: How to Change Your mind.**

https://www.amazon.com/dp/B07F68938F

# CONCLUSION

Now you know everything that you need to begin your journey. Your destination: your dream life. You have an action plan. You know the techniques and methods. All you need are the will and the action. If your dreams are more specific than the general themes we have talked about such as money, love, or health, just apply the same steps to your particular wish and you will have your action plan. The principles are the same. You can attract anything you want because you are the creator, not the observer, of your reality.

Before you begin, take some time to be alone in silence. Reflect and practice introspection. Think about your thoughts and beliefs. Become aware of your emotions. Get close to your inner being again.

After a few days of doing that, you will be ready to think about your future and what you want from life. Write about it. Writing is exceptionally efficient in getting your thoughts in order. If you are feeling especially crafty, you can make a vision board. You will need pictures of what you want to make you feel as if you already have them. This could include pictures of particular things you desire but could also form a bigger picture of the lifestyle that you want. You can use photos, pictures from magazines, or even drawings if you are artistic. Place your vision board in a place where you will see it often. The principle with pictures is the same as with words: your subconscious does not care if you are looking at your brand new car or just a piece of paper with an image on it.

Now you've got it! The point is to feel awesome. That way, all the pieces of the puzzle will come into place. When you are on a high vibration, you will attract more things which will make your life more enjoyable. So, what are you waiting for? Grab your wishes and have fun! The Law of Attraction will be your friend and companion on this magnificent self-growth journey.

Made in United States
Orlando, FL
29 August 2023

36508835R00026